World Cities

ROME

Nicola Barber

*Special photography
by Chris Fairclough*

Belitha Press

First published in the UK in 2000 by

 Belitha Press Limited
London House, Great Eastern Wharf,
Parkgate Road, London SW11 4NQ

ISBN 1 84138 119 5

British Library Cataloguing in Publication Data
for this book is available from the British Library.

Printed in Singapore

Editor Stephanie Turnbull
Designer Helen James
Photographer Chris Fairclough
Map illustrator Lorraine Harrison
Picture researcher Kathy Lockley
Consultant Katy Elphinstone, The British Council, Rome

Additional images
AKG London 8b, 10t, 11t, 36t, 40t, /Erich Lessing 10b, 36b, /Jean-Louis
Nou 9b, /Museo Capitolino 8t, /National Museum of Archaeology, Naples
9t; Bridgeman Art Library London /Giraudon 20t, /Private Collection 40b;
Colorsport 35t; Corbis /c.Hulton-Deutsch Collection 11b, /c.Massimo
Listri 24b; Mary Evans Picture Library 23b; Ronald Grant Archive 41t;
Robert Harding Picture Library 37t, 38tl, 39t; Ikona /c.AFE/photo Mario
Tursi 43cr, /c.AFE/photo Riccardo Abbondanza 21b, /c.Agenzia Sintesi/
Remo Casilli 39b, /c.Agenzia Sintesi/Carlo Lannutti 35b, 38br, /c.Agenzia
Sintesi/Remo Casilli 42b, /c.Agenzia Sintesi/Stefano Carofei 43bl;
Rex Features 4l, 27b, 37b, 41br, 41cr; Frank Spooner Pictures 15t.

Words in **bold** are explained in the glossary on pages 46 and 47.

CONTENTS

INTRODUCTION

Rome is the capital city of Italy. It is also the capital of the region of Lazio. Rome lies in central Italy, on the River Tiber. In ancient times Rome was the centre of a powerful empire. It is still a great historic and cultural capital, visited every year by millions of tourists from all over the world. The modern city covers 1,500 square kilometres and is home to nearly three million people. The Vatican, an independent **state**, lies within the city of Rome.

Seven Hills

Ancient Rome was founded alongside the River Tiber near a small island called Tiber Island. The city grew up on seven hills on the east bank of the Tiber – the Aventine, Capitoline, Celian, Esquiline, Palatine, Quirinal and Viminal. Today, the city extends far beyond these original seven hills. The Vatican City State is on the west bank of the Tiber on another small hill called Monte Vaticano.

▲ Tiber Island, in the River Tiber. The island is linked with the north bank by the oldest bridge in Rome, built in 62 BC.

People enjoy a warm ➤ evening by Neptune's Fountain in the **Piazza** Navona. The square has three fountains. The largest is the Fountain of the Four Rivers (see page 17).

FAST FACTS
ROME

STATUS
Capital of Italy and of the region of Lazio

AREA
1,500 square kilometres

POPULATION
2,653,000 (1997)

GOVERNING BODY
Council (Commune di Roma)
led by a mayor

CLIMATE
Temperatures average 20 to 30°C in summer
and 10°C in winter

TIME ZONE
Greenwich Mean Time plus 1 hour
(2 hours in summer)

CURRENCY
1 lira (plural lire) = 100 centesimi

OFFICIAL LANGUAGE
Italian

▲ The Palazzo Senatorio is in the Piazza del Campidoglio. It houses the offices of the mayor of Rome.

Capital city

Rome became the capital of Italy in 1870. The population of Rome at that time was only 200,000, but 30 years later it had more than doubled. It has continued to grow ever since as more and more people have moved to Rome from the surrounding areas.

Pilgrims and visitors

Rome has been a magnet for **pilgrims** and tourists for centuries. Over 25 million visitors are expected to travel to Rome during the year 2000. The city has many attractions – the ruined remains of Ancient Rome, beautiful **Renaissance** palaces and fine museums and galleries. People also come to visit the Vatican, the centre of the Roman Catholic Church.

MAP OF THE CITY

This map shows central Rome as it is today. Many of the buildings, parks and other places mentioned in the book are marked.

1. Vatican City
2. St Peter's
3. Vatican Museums
4. Sistine Chapel
5. St Peter's Square
6. Villa Doria Pamphilj
7. Janiculum Hill
8. Botanical Gardens
9. Trastevere
10. Castle St Angelo
11. St Angelo Bridge
12. **Piazza** Navona
13. Pantheon
14. Ghetto
15. Tiber Island
16. Aventine Hill
17. Piazza Venezia
18. Victor Emmanuel Monument
19. Capitoline Museums
20. Capitoline Hill
21. Forum
22. Farnese Gardens
23. Palatine Hill
24. Colosseum
25. Celian Hill
26. Spanish Steps
27. Villa Medici
28. Villa Borghese
29. Temple of Diana
30. Trevi Fountain
31. Quirinal Hill
32. Viminal Hill
33. National Museum of Rome
34. Church of Saint Maria Maggiore
35. Esquiline Hill

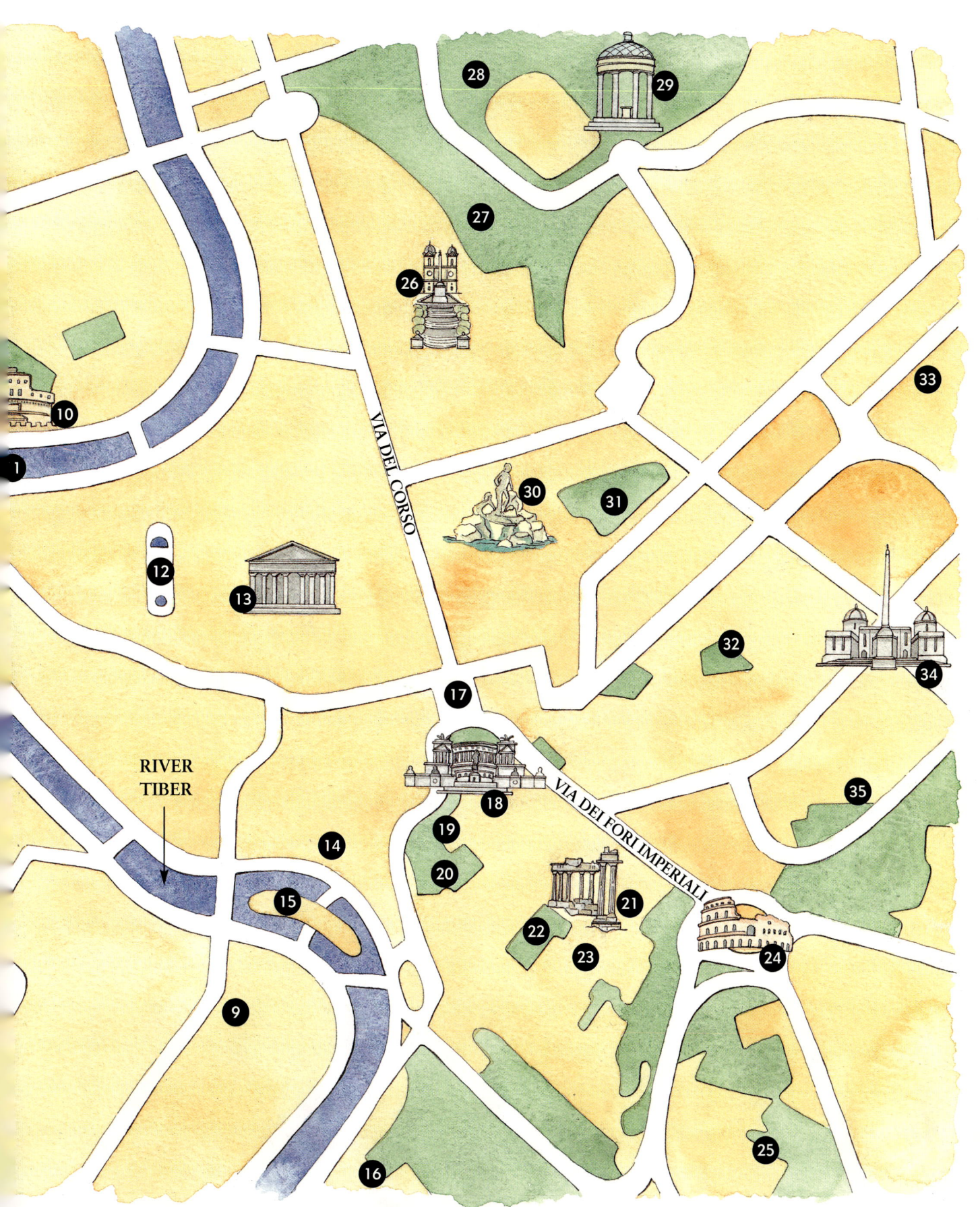

RIVER
TIBER

VIA DEL CORSO

VIA DEI FORI IMPERIALI

ANCIENT ROME

According to the Ancient Roman historian, Livy, Rome was founded in 753 BC by Romulus. Livy's account of early Rome is based on legend, although we know that there was a real settlement on the site of present-day Rome by the 8th century BC. As this settlement grew it came under the rule of the **Etruscans**. It was probably Etruscans who drained marshes between the seven hills (see page 4) to create the **Forum** (see page 16).

ROMULUS AND REMUS

According to legend, twin brothers Romulus and Remus were abandoned at birth on the banks of the River Tiber. A she-wolf found the twins and cared for them (above) until they were rescued by a shepherd. When they grew up, the brothers decided to start a settlement on the hills above the river. They quarrelled about who should be king. Romulus climbed to the top of the Palatine, while Remus ran up the Aventine. Six vultures flew over the Aventine, which Remus thought was a sign that he would be king – but then 12 vultures flew over Romulus' hill. Romulus later murdered Remus and became the first king of Rome.

The Republic of Rome

In 509 BC Livy states that the Romans overthrew the Etruscan rulers and set up a **Republic**. This was run by officials called **consuls**, who were elected every year. Over the following centuries the Republic became more and more powerful as the Romans took over other tribes, including the Etruscans. The power of the Roman Republic brought it into conflict with the Carthaginians, who controlled much of North Africa and Spain. The wars between Rome and Carthage, known as the **Punic Wars**, lasted for 120 years.

This painting shows the Carthaginian ➤ leader, Hannibal, leading his troops across the Alps to attack the Romans.

Patricians and Plebeians

The elected consuls in the Roman Republic were guided by a council called the Senate. Only the richest people in Rome could vote for the consuls, or be in the Senate. These powerful people were called patricians. The ordinary people of Rome were known as plebeians. In 494 BC the plebeians rebelled against patrician rule. The result was the election of two plebeian representatives, called tribunes, and a written code of law called the Twelve Tables, displayed in the Forum.

Imperial Rome

Republican Rome came to an end in 27 BC and the **Roman Empire** began. The first emperor was Augustus, who greatly improved the city. He divided it into 14 areas, each one run by officials. He set up a fire brigade and a police force. He constructed many buildings, boasting that he transformed a city made of brick into one made of marble. Later emperors continued to build in Rome and to expand the Empire. During the 1st and early 2nd century AD Rome was a magnificent city, with a population of more than one million.

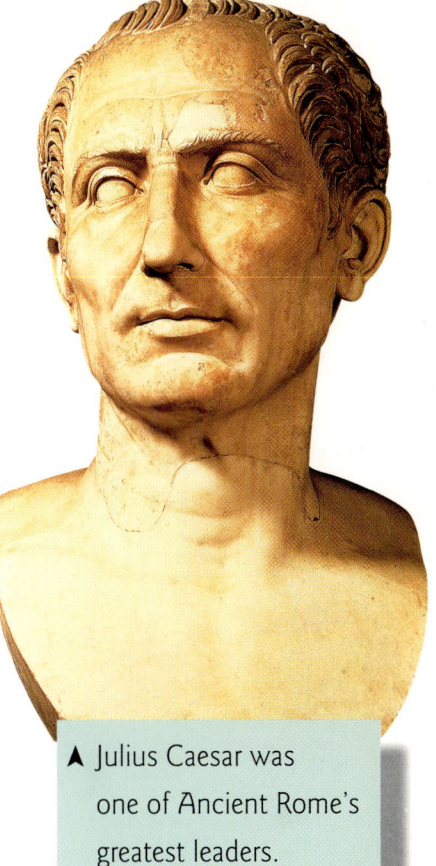

▲ Julius Caesar was one of Ancient Rome's greatest leaders. He came to power in 49 BC. Five years later he was murdered on his way to a meeting in the Senate.

▲ A maid brushes her mistress' hair. This stone sculpture is from Tunisia in North Africa, part of the Roman Empire.

The fall of the Empire

In the 3rd century AD the Romans found it increasingly hard to control their huge empire. Foreign tribes were threatening to invade and there was a risk of **civil war**. To try to protect the city, Emperor Aurelius built a huge wall, the Aurelian Wall, around Rome. Nevertheless the city was raided and looted in 410 by the **Visigoths** and in 455 by the **Vandals**. In 476 the western half of the Roman Empire collapsed, completely overrun by foreign tribes.

AFTER THE ROMAN EMPIRE

After the collapse of the Roman Empire, Rome fell into decline. There were many invasions and the population of the city fell. At the same time Rome became a centre of the Christian Church, headed by the **pope**.

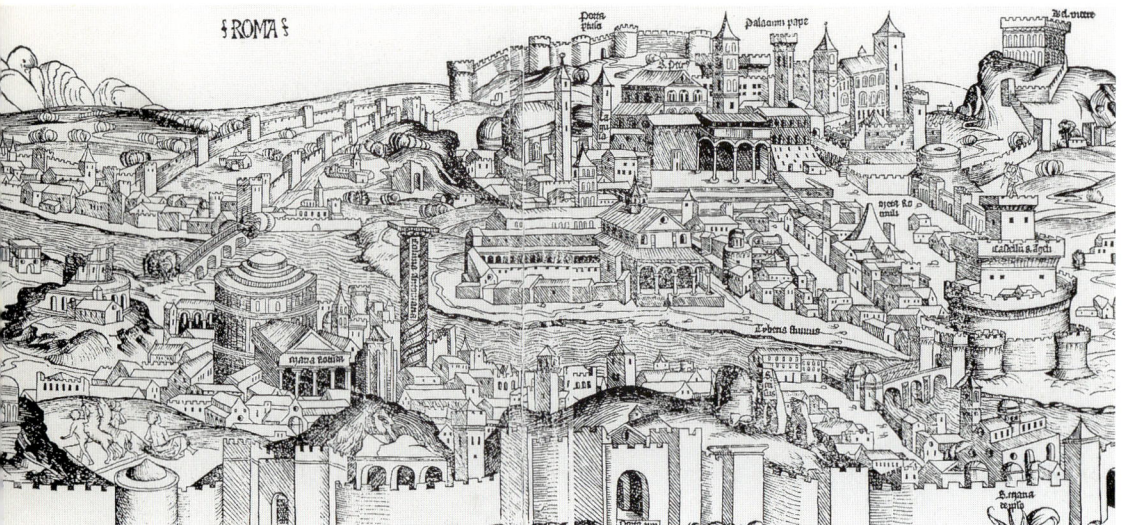

◄ This view of Rome was drawn in 1493. On the right is Castle St Angelo (see page 13) and on the far left is the edge of the Colosseum (see page 16).

▲ Sixtus IV was pope from 1471-84. He founded the Sistine Chapel (see page 37).

Families at war

Rome was a lawless and derelict city in the 14th century. The city's water supply was cut off, its buildings were ravaged by fire, earthquake and war and its population was reduced to less than 20,000 by the **Black Death**. Rome's noble families (see page 14) waged war against each other, their followers running riot through the ruined buildings and streets of the city.

Renaissance Rome

The reign of Pope Martin V (1417-31) marked the start of a new era in Rome's history. Pope Martin began to clean up and restore the crumbling, filthy city. His reign was also the start of **papal** rule in Rome, which lasted until 1870. It was Pope Nicholas V (1447-55) who brought the **Renaissance** to Rome. He founded the Vatican Library (see page 37) and planned the rebuilding of St Peter's (see page 12). Later popes continued to bring scholars and artists from all over Italy, turning Rome once again into a magnificent city.

▲ In 1527 the armies of Charles V of Spain attacked Rome and **sacked** the city. They burned and destroyed buildings and stole many precious works of art. The pope fled to Castle St Angelo (see page 13).

Invasions and independence

In 1798 French troops commanded by **Napoleon** marched into Rome and took control of the city. Rome became a **Republic** once again, but papal rule was restored in the city in 1814. In 1861 the many small Italian **states** were combined to make one country. Rome became the capital of the unified Italy in 1870. The pope at that time, Pius XI, did not want to be part of this country, so he shut himself inside the Vatican. Later popes did the same until, nearly 60 years later, the Vatican became an independent state (see page 12).

▼ Benito Mussolini marching at the head of his troops. This photograph was taken in 1935 outside the Venezia Palace in Rome.

Fascism and beyond

After 1870 the government of the newly unified Italy made its home in Rome. Then in 1922 the **Fascists**, led by **Benito Mussolini**, marched on the city and gained power. Mussolini took Italy into the **Second World War** in 1940 on the side of the Germans. After several Italian defeats the German leader, Adolf Hitler, sent German troops to occupy Rome. Mussolini was finally captured and killed in 1945. After the end of the war, the Italian people voted for their country to become a Republic.

THE VATICAN CITY STATE

The Vatican is the world's smallest nation. It has an area of 0.44 square kilometres and a population of about 700. It lies within the city of Rome, but is an independent **state**, with its own post office, telephone network, currency and banking system. The head of state is the **pope**.

Early history

In 67 AD Saint Peter (see page 24) was executed on a spot west of the Tiber. In 90 AD a small **shrine** was built there, and later, in the 320s, a **basilica** was erected on the site of the shrine. This was the first St Peter's. In the 9th century Pope Leo IV built a high wall that went around the Vatican and Castle St Angelo to protect St Peter's from attack. After the **sack** of Rome in 1527 (see page 11), the pope moved to the east side of the river. Later popes also lived here until 1870 when Rome became capital of a united Italy and the pope once more retreated behind the safety of the walls of the Vatican (see page 11).

▲ St Peter's Basilica is the centre of the Roman Catholic Church, visited by thousands of **pilgrims** every year.

▲ The Vatican has its own special stamps. These stamps show famous popes from the past as well as details from St Peter's.

The Lateran Treaty

In 1929 the **Lateran Treaty** was agreed between Pope Pius XI and the **Fascist** leader, **Benito Mussolini** (see page 11). This treaty made the Vatican an independent state with the pope as its head. The government also paid the Vatican compensation for the loss of **papal** lands in 1870 and ruled that its people did not have to pay taxes.

◄ The impressive view across the square in front of St Peter's. The **obelisk** in the centre was brought to Rome from Egypt in 37 AD.

Choosing a pope

When the pope dies, a new pope is chosen as quickly as possible. This is done in secret inside the Vatican. People outside watch the chimney of the Sistine Chapel. If white smoke comes out of the chimney, this means a new pope has been chosen.

The Swiss Guards

The Vatican has its own private army to protect its inhabitants. The members of this force are all male, between 19 and 30 years of age, Catholic and Swiss. They are called the Swiss Guards and they wear bright red, yellow and blue uniforms, said to have been designed by **Michelangelo**. The Swiss Guards were brought to the Vatican by Pope Julius II in 1506 after the pope had been impressed by their skill in battle. They were used as a fighting force until 1825, after which they became the pope's force of bodyguards.

THE SECRET PASSAGE

When Pope Leo IV built the wall around the Vatican, he also created a small corridor, the *passetto*, between the Vatican buildings and Castle St Angelo. This corridor provided a useful means of escape to the castle if the Vatican buildings were under attack. It was used by Pope Alexander VI in 1494 to flee the invading French, and again by Pope Clement VII in 1527 when the Vatican was **besieged** by the armies of Charles V.

▲ A Swiss Guard on duty at one of the entrances to St Peter's. Guards also watch over the priceless contents of the Vatican Museums.

THE PEOPLE OF ROME

When Rome became the capital of the newly united Italy in 1870, its population was 200,000. It was only the third largest Italian city after Milan in the north and Naples in the south. The population soon increased and by 1936 Rome was the largest city in Italy.

▲ Everyday life on the Via del Corso. Many Romans get around the city on motorbikes and mopeds (see page 28).

Noble families

Some Roman families have existed for many generations. The Colonna **dynasty** claims to go back as far as the **Etruscans** (see page 9). Other noble families such as the Corsini, Orsini and Aldobrandini became powerful during the **Renaissance**. These families kept private armies and they often fought each other. Many **popes** came from these mighty dynasties.

Keeping up appearances

Visitors to Italy are often amazed at how stylish the Italian people are. Most Romans take great pride in their appearance, and try to look their best at all times. This is known in Italy as *la bella figura* ('keeping up appearances'). Appearance is so important that in 1989 the city of Rome introduced a law allowing the police to fine anyone in a public place who is not properly dressed – for example a man without a shirt.

▲ Shoppers on the Via Frattina, one of the stylish shopping streets near the Spanish Steps, in the historical centre of Rome.

SEEING THE POPE

Millions of visitors come to Rome to see just one person – the pope. Pope John Paul appears once a week at noon on Sunday, at the balcony of the **papal** apartments in St Peter's Square (above). He also holds a weekly audience, attended by up to 8,000 people, in a special hall in the Vatican.

Trastevere

The Trastevere area of Rome is on the west bank of the Tiber, opposite the historical centre. In ancient times this was the area where **immigrants** lived, including the first Jews to settle in Rome. Most modern-day immigrants to Rome come from Africa, particularly Algeria, Tunisia, Nigeria and Magreb.

A day in the life

Romans have a reputation for being relaxed, fun-loving and a bit arrogant! A saying from Milan goes: 'In Milan we work; in Rome they eat' which sums up (and exaggerates) the view of many northern Italians about Romans. The traditional Roman working day has a long lunch break, in which people go home for a big meal, though this is less common now. In the evening many Romans like to take a stroll. This is called the *passeggiata* and it is a time both to see and be seen.

Jewish Rome

There have been Jews in Rome for over 2,000 years. In 1556 Pope Paul IV forced all Jews in the city to live in a walled-off area that became known as the Ghetto. Jewish people were **persecuted** until the unification of Italy in 1870 (see page 11), when the squalid streets in the Ghetto were rebuilt. Many Jewish Romans died in **concentration camps** in Germany during the **Second World War**. Today, Jews still live in the Ghetto area, where there are many shops selling **kosher** food.

▲ A gypsy woman begging for money in a Rome street. Her sign tells her story: 'I am a poor grandmother... I need medicines...'

ARCHITECTURE

Evidence of Rome's long and colourful history is everywhere. Ancient ruins, medieval churches, **Renaissance** palaces and modern apartments sit side by side. Layers of ancient buildings lie deep beneath the streets of the modern city.

Ancient remains

Most of the magnificent buildings of Ancient Rome are now ruins. The **Forum** was the centre of Ancient Rome, a bustling place full of law courts, offices and temples. Today all that remain are a few walls, columns and the layouts of the floors, yet they still give us an idea of how impressive the area once was. Some of Rome's ancient buildings still stand, including the Colosseum (see page 34) and the Pantheon. The Pantheon is the city's best-preserved ancient building. It was built by Emperor Hadrian from 118-128 AD as a temple to the 12 most important Roman gods.

▲ The interior of the Pantheon is a spectacular sight. The huge domed ceiling has a hole in the top to let light into the building.

▲ Ruins in the Roman Forum. The Forum was rebuilt many times in the Ancient Roman era. Many stones were taken to build new structures.

St Peter's

The present **basilica** of St Peter's dates from 1506, when Pope Julius II ordered the old church to be torn down and a new one to be built in its place. Building work continued for more than a century. In 1547 **Michelangelo** took over as chief architect and designed the magnificent dome. It was the largest brick dome ever constructed. Inside St Peter's is a beautiful **canopy** called the *baldacchino*. This was designed by **Gian Lorenzo Bernini** in the 17th century and was made of bronze taken from the roof of the Pantheon.

Fountains and obelisks

Rome is a city of many elaborate fountains and tall **obelisks.** One of Rome's best-known fountains is the Trevi Fountain, the largest in the city. Some fountains stand in the centre of grand squares, such as the Fountain of the Four Rivers in the **Piazza** Navona, designed by Bernini. Some of Rome's obelisks date from ancient times, carried back by victorious armies from parts of the **Roman Empire** (see page 13).

▲ The Trevi Fountain was completed in 1762. It shows Neptune, the Roman god of the sea, surrounded by mythical sea creatures.

◀ The Colosseum lies at the eastern end of the Forum. It was built by Emperor Vespasian to provide entertainment for the people of Rome (see page 34).

Fascist plans

Mussolini (see page 11) had many plans for Rome, including building a huge Palace of Fascism and clearing away large areas of the medieval city. Most of the plans came to nothing, although a huge road – the Via dei Fori Imperiali – was built in central Rome. Mussolini also began a development called **EUR** on the outskirts of Rome. This was intended to mark the 20th anniversary of his march on Rome in 1922, but work stopped as the **Second World War** began.

▲ Part of the EUR complex. In the background is the huge Building of the Civilization of Work, nicknamed the 'square Colosseum'.

OPEN SPACES

Rome is one of the greenest cities in Europe, with many beautiful parks and gardens. They provide a refuge from the traffic and noise of the city and offer welcome shade in the heat of the summer.

Villa Borghese

The most central of Rome's large open spaces is the park of the Villa Borghese. Both the villa and the park were designed in the early 17th century for Cardinal Scipio Borghese. The park was originally laid out as a formal garden, but it was altered in the 18th century to look like natural parkland. It became a public park in 1902. It is a popular place for jogging, picnicking and rowing on the lake. It houses a zoo, a children's cinema and temples such as the elegant Temple of Diana.

▲ A temple in the park of the Villa Borghese. This temple is on an island in the park's lake.

▲ A view across Rome from the Janiculum Hill. The huge white building is a monument to Victor Emmanuel II, first king of unified Italy.

The best view in Rome?

One of the best views across Rome is from the top of the Janiculum Hill on the west bank of the River Tiber. The park also contains several fascinating monuments, including a lighthouse.

Villa Doria Pamphilj

Rome's largest public park is outside the city centre. The park of the Villa Doria Pamphilj was laid out in 1652 for Prince Camillo Pamphilj, nephew of Pope Innocent X. It was bought by the Italian government in the 1960s and became a public park.

BOTANICAL GARDENS

Rome's Botanical Gardens are at the foot
of the Janiculum Hill, in the grounds of
the Corsini Palace. In 1883 the grounds
of this palace were given to the University
of Rome and the Botanical Gardens were
set up. Today there are over 7,000 species
of plant in the Gardens. There is a garden
full of scented plants for the enjoyment
of blind people, as well as an area where
all kinds of medicinal herbs are grown.

The Farnese Gardens

Not surprisingly, many of Rome's parks and gardens contain
ruins of ancient buildings. The Farnese Gardens on the Palatine
Hill were built in the ruined remains of the ancient palace
of Emperor Tiberius. The ruins were filled in by Cardinal
Alessandro Farnese, grandson of Pope Paul III, to create the
first botanical gardens in Europe. Today, some parts of Tiberius'
palace have been re-excavated, but you can still walk through
the park's rose gardens and along its tree-lined avenues.

▲ The Pincio Gardens
are a popular and
fashionable place to
stroll, jog or skate.
The park has many
wide, leafy avenues
and an expensive
café and restaurant.

▲ The wonderful view over the Vatican
Gardens. These beautiful gardens also
contain a grotto, a specially built cave.

The Vatican Gardens

Visitors to the Vatican can glimpse
its large gardens from the dome of
St Peter's, or from parts of the
Vatican Museums. The gardens are
private and people have to book
days in advance to reserve a place
on a guided tour. Hidden away
in these gardens is a beautiful
summerhouse and the large Eagle
Fountain, topped by the eagle that
appears on the Borghese family crest.

HOMES AND HOUSING

The people of modern Rome live in a wide variety of homes, from spacious villas to modern apartment blocks.

Fire in Ancient Rome

More than one million people lived in Ancient Rome. Public areas of the city were magnificent, but housing areas for the plebeians (see page 9) were dirty and overcrowded. Apartment blocks towered six storeys high on either side of dark, narrow streets. These buildings often collapsed or, because people used open stoves for cooking, caught fire. In 64 AD a huge fire burned down a large part of the city. After this Emperor Nero made new rules for building. Much of Rome was rebuilt, but poor people continued to live in noisy, cramped conditions.

▲ This painting shows the fire that destroyed much of Rome in 64 AD. Some people think that Emperor Nero started the fire deliberately to clear the way for his own building projects.

Rome in ruins

As the **Roman Empire** collapsed so did Rome. In 455 the **Vandals** attacked the city (see page 9) and caused a huge amount of damage to its monuments and buildings. Earthquakes and further invasions left much of Rome in ruins. By the 14th century the city of Rome was described by the Italian poet Petrarch as a 'shapeless heap of ruins'.

◄ One of the many narrow, cobbled streets in Trastevere. People in these houses sometimes string their washing lines across the street.

Planning the capital

After Rome became the capital of Italy in 1870, the city's population more than doubled in 30 years. Many government officials moved to Rome, as well as thousands of people from the poor south who came to find work as labourers. This led to a building boom in Rome. Some of the worst slum areas in the centre of the city, such as the Ghetto (see page 15), were cleared away and rebuilt. New residential areas were created outside the city walls. However a **stock market crash** in 1887 brought a sudden end to the building boom and houses were left half-completed across the city.

▲ These modern apartment blocks are in Rome's southern suburbs. Shutters keep out the fierce heat in summer.

▲ In the suburbs of Rome there are many large villas, home to the city's richest inhabitants.

Living in Rome

Today, Rome has spread far beyond the original city walls. Testaccio and Trastevere are traditionally poorer areas, but have become lively and fashionable places to live. Rich Romans have apartments in the historical centre of Rome or in the Parioli area, to the north of the Villa Borghese. Many people live in unplanned developments in the suburbs, called *borgate*, which were often built haphazardly and without any thought about access to services such as transport or shopping facilities.

EDUCATION

All Italian children go to school between the ages of six and fourteen. There are now plans to change this so that children will have to attend school from the age of five to fifteen or even sixteen. Most Italians go to **state**-run schools, although there are some private schools, usually run by the Roman Catholic Church.

Going to school

Although children don't have to go to school until the age of six, many Roman children attend nursery schools in the city, starting from three years old. At six they move to elementary school, then at the age of eleven they go to middle school. When children are fourteen, they must decide whether to leave school or to continue with their education.

▲ Children arriving at school. Some schools are closed in the afternoon and children have to go to classes on Saturdays instead.

◄ Children hard at work in an elementary school in Rome. They study a wide range of subjects and are usually given about an hour of homework each day.

Secondary education

There are many types of secondary schools in Rome. Some are technical schools which train pupils for careers in industry, commerce or agriculture. Others teach science, classical education and the arts. Pupils can also go to teacher-training schools. Most examinations are oral – based on the spoken word – rather than written. Even university degrees are taken as oral exams, although students must also write a detailed essay.

 The University of Rome. This part of the huge building houses the university concert hall as well as a library and conference rooms.

The University of Rome

Rome's university was founded in 1303 by Pope Boniface VIII. Until 1935 it was based in the Palazzo Sapienza in the centre of the city. In 1935 the main part of the university moved to a new campus in the Termini area, although there are university buildings scattered around the city. Today about 189,000 students attend the university. Most Italians go to their local university, so they live at home while completing their degree.

THE PRIX DE ROME

The Prix de Rome was a group of prizes created by the French king Louis XIV. It allowed French students to live in Rome and study at the French Academy in the magnificent Villa Medici (left). Some of these students were famous, such as the artists Jacques-Louis David and Jean-Auguste Ingres and the composers Hector Berlioz, Georges Bizet and Claude Debussy.

RELIGION

 Rome was one of the earliest centres of Christianity and today it is the heart of the Roman Catholic Church. Although the **pope** no longer governs the city, as popes did from the 15th to the 19th centuries (see pages 10-11), the influence of the Catholic Church is still strong.

▲ The church of Saint Maria sopra Minerva is on the site of an ancient temple to Minerva, the Roman goddess of wisdom. The church interior is richly decorated.

Early Christianity

The first Christians came to Rome soon after the crucifixion of Jesus Christ. The Roman rulers were suspicious of this religion and they **persecuted** and killed many Christians. In 42 AD Peter – one of Jesus' followers – arrived in Rome with another Christian named Paul. Peter became the first Bishop of Rome (pope). Both Peter and Paul were later put to death for their beliefs. In 313 Christians were finally allowed to worship in the city and in 380 Christianity became the official religion of the **Roman Empire.**

CATACOMBS

Early Christians in Rome often buried their dead in underground tunnels called catacombs (left). This was because burying dead bodies within the city walls was not allowed and burial plots outside the walls were very expensive. After Christianity became the official religion of the Roman Empire, the catacombs were important places of pilgrimage as many saints were buried there. More than 300 kilometres of catacombs exist beneath modern Rome.

A centre of pilgrimage

Rome has been an important destination for **pilgrims** ever since the earliest days of Christianity. In 1300 Pope Boniface VIII declared the first Holy Year, a special celebration which brought thousands of extra pilgrims to Rome. The streets were packed with visitors eager to see the **shrines** and famous **relics**. This and following Holy Years brought huge profits to the Vatican and to the people of Rome.

▲ A group of nuns in St Peter's Square (see page 13). Pilgrims come to Rome all year round, though Easter is the busiest time.

Unbelieving Rome

Rome may be a city packed with churches and pilgrims, but the Roman people themselves are not necessarily church-goers. Only a small percentage of the city's population attends **Mass** regularly. A local saying goes: 'Faith is made here but believed elsewhere.'

The popes in France

Over the years there have been challenges to Rome's position as centre of the Catholic Church. In 1309 the French pope Clement V moved the **papal** court to Avignon in the south of France. For 68 years Avignon was the centre of the Catholic Church until Pope Gregory XI returned to Rome in 1377. After his death people argued and fought over who should become pope. This time is known as the **Great Schism**. It came to an end in 1417 when Pope Martin V was elected and brought the court back to Rome in 1420.

▲ Muslims also live in Rome. Many worship in this mosque in the Parioli district. The building was completed in 1992.

INDUSTRY AND FINANCE

Rome is Italy's centre of government as well as a major tourist attraction. Compared with cities in the north of Italy, there is little industry in Rome.

Religious capital

When Rome became the capital of Italy in 1870, the city was important as the centre of the Roman Catholic Church, but not as a leader of finance or industry. People in Rome relied on the Church, which made money from the thousands of **pilgrims** that came to the city each year. The industrial and commercial centres of Italy were in northern cities such as Milan and Turin.

◀ The tourist industry in Rome is booming. Souvenir stalls are found near every tourist attraction.

▲ Italy is famous for its fashion industry. These clothes were created by the well-known Roman designer Valentino Garavani (see page 31).

The heart of Italy

Although other cities may have had better claims to become the capital of Italy, Rome was, in the words of the revolutionary **Giuseppe Mazzini**, the 'natural centre of Italian unity'. With its long and fascinating history and its magnificent monuments and buildings, Rome was a powerful symbol of Italy's past. Rome's geographical position, in the centre of the country and linking the rich north with the poorer southern regions, was also ideal.

FINANCE

Rome has its own *borsa* (**stock exchange**) but it is not as important as the stock exchange in Milan, which is still Italy's main financial centre. Rome continues to be a centre of government and administration. Almost two thirds of Rome's working population is employed by the government and other agencies such as the United Nations Food and Agriculture Organization (FAO).

▲ This grand building is the Treasury, on Via XX Settembre. It houses the government's finance department.

Industry in Rome

After unification, the government discouraged industry in Rome. Nevertheless some industry has developed. Building and renovation work provides jobs for many thousands of people, especially during the run-up to the Jubilee 2000 (see page 42). In the south of the city, Cinecittà employs people in the film-making business (see page 34). The main industrial area is in the northwest of the city where there are food-processing and textile factories. Newer industries are in the south and east of the city and include printing, engineering and the production of chemicals and plastics.

▲ This is Archbishop Paul Marcinkus, the chairman of the Vatican Bank who was accused of fraud in the 1980s.

Scandal in the Vatican

The Vatican has its own financial institution, called the Vatican Bank. In the late 1980s scandal erupted when Italian judges issued a warrant for the arrest of the chairman of the Vatican Bank and two other bank officials. They were wanted in connection with fraud charges. However, lawyers argued successfully that under the terms of the **Lateran Treaty** (see page 12) the Italian **state** could not arrest citizens of the Vatican.

GETTING AROUND

There are over two million vehicles on Rome's roads.
Many streets in the historic city centre are now closed to traffic,
but elsewhere cars pack the roads, causing terrible congestion and pollution.

▲ Cars, taxis, motorbikes and mopeds on a busy street during the rush hour in Rome.

Angry wasps

Many Romans avoid the worst of the traffic jams by travelling around the city on scooters or mopeds. Bicycles are less common, as the combination of heavy traffic and narrow, steep streets makes cycling a difficult task.

Buses and trams

The main methods of public transport in Rome are buses and trams. The city transport authority runs the city buses and eight tram lines. Older buses and trams are painted bright orange, while the newest models are green. The buses, trams and Metro work as one system and passengers can buy one ticket that covers all travel within Rome.

Crossing the road

Romans are famous for their speedy driving, and visitors to Rome find life as a pedestrian both frightening and intimidating. Romans, however, know that pedestrians have right of way at zebra crossings so long as they cross the road with purpose and make eye contact with oncoming drivers!

These smart trams are part of the ➤ new express tram service that links the suburbs to the centre of Rome.

On the Metro

Rome has a small Metro system with only two lines. Line A runs from Ottaviano in the northwest to Battistini in the southeast. Line B runs from Rebibbia in the northeast to Laurentina in the south. The lines cross at the main railway station in Rome, Termini, and are used mainly by **commuters** to travel in and out of Rome. Plans to build more Metro lines have failed in the past, though construction on a third line has now begun.

A typical Metro sign on Line B of the underground network. A single Metro ticket lasts for 75 minutes and can also be used on the city's buses and trams.

◀ A Pendolino train at Rome's main station, Termini. The fast and luxurious Pendolino service runs between the main cities of Italy.

THE PATRON SAINT OF DRIVERS

Roman drivers have their very own **patron saint** – Francesca Romana. Francesca cared for the poor during times of famine in the 15th century. In modern Rome, on their patron's special day – 9 March – drivers bring their cars as close as possible to the church of Saint Francesca Romana to be blessed.

Getting to Rome

Rome has two international airports. The main airport, Leonardo da Vinci, is usually known as Fiumicino. It lies about 30 kilometres to the southwest of the city and is linked to the city centre by a fast train that runs to Termini station. Most scheduled flights land at Fiumicino, which is the fifth busiest airport in Europe (after London, Amsterdam, Paris and Frankfurt). Rome's second airport, Ciampino, is 15 kilometres south of the city and handles most charter flights.

SHOPS AND MARKETS

In ancient times, craftworkers from all over the **Roman Empire** supplied Rome's wealthy inhabitants with fine and exotic goods. Today, shops in Rome still place the emphasis on quality and style. The city is full of small shops selling designer clothes, art, antiques and delicious food.

Superstores

Many people in Rome still buy from small, specialist shops, so there are only a few large shopping centres in the city. Rome's major shopping malls are Cinecittà Due Centro Commerciale, which contains over 100 shops, La Metro, which sells everything from computers to food, and the newly-opened I Granai. The most upmarket department stores are La Rinascente and Coin.

▲ This food shop on the Campo de' Fiori specializes in dairy products such as butter and cheese, as well as foreign foods.

Markets

Almost every area in Rome has its own local market selling fresh foods. Daily markets such as those held in the Campo de' Fiori and Testaccio Square have magnificent displays of fruit and vegetables, meat and fish. Many markets sell wonderful flowers and plants, as well as kitchen equipment, clothes and shoes. There is also a market that specializes in second-hand books and antique prints. For second-hand clothes, Romans go to the market on the Via Sannio. The largest flea market in Rome is held on Sundays near the Portese Gate in the Trastevere area.

▲ Bargaining at the flea market near the Portese Gate. This market sells almost everything, from clothes to pets.

Alta moda

Italy is one of the world leaders in *alta moda* (high-class fashions). Many of the country's leading fashion designers are based in Milan, but some famous designers work in Rome, including Valentino and Fendi. All the big names in Italian fashion have boutiques in Rome, including Armani, Gucci and Versace.

Street fairs

Rome is famous for its street fairs. At Christmas, special Italian gifts are sold at the Natale Oggi fair held at **EUR**, and from mid-December until 6 January a traditional fair is held in the **Piazza** Navona. In the summer, the Expo Tevere opens along the banks of the River Tiber between the St Angelo and Cavour bridges. Stalls sell traditional crafts as well as pasta, olive oil and wine. There are also antiques fairs that take place along the Via dei Coronari and Via dell'Orso, the roads that form the centre of Rome's antique trade.

▲ Furniture restorers at work in the open air. Rome has a long history of producing expertly-crafted goods.

Shopping streets

In the centre of Rome, shops selling similar goods are often found in one street or a group of streets. Designer fashions are sold mostly in the area of the Via Condotti, near the Spanish Steps. For antiques and modern art, shoppers head for the expensive galleries in Via del Babuino. The best place to look for delicious food is along the Via della Croce, which is packed full of delicatessens, cafés and bars.

◄ The Ghezzi shop sells all kinds of religious objects such as icons, statues, candlesticks and oil and wine holders.

FOOD AND DRINK

Good-quality meat, fish, vegetables and fish are all sold daily in Rome's markets. Roman cuisine is based around delicious, fresh ingredients prepared in a simple way. Romans take food very seriously, both at home and in restaurants, and love to eat out with friends.

▲ This shop has a tempting display of *antipasti* (appetizers) made of aubergines, tomatoes, olives and cheese.

Pasta and pizza

As in the rest of Italy, pasta forms an important part of the Roman diet. *Spaghetti alla carbonara* (spaghetti with bacon, cheese and egg) is a famous pasta dish that was created in Rome. This dish uses a traditional Roman cheese – *pecorino romano* – which is made from ewe's milk. There are also many pizzerias in the city offering Roman pizzas, which are rolled very thin and baked in a wood-burning stove.

◀ A delicious, thin, Roman pizza, served straight from the oven. Pizza can also be bought by the slice at fast food stalls.

THE FIFTH QUARTER

Many traditional Roman recipes are based around the *quinto quarto* (fifth quarter). This refers to offal – an animal's head, tail, liver, kidneys and so on. This tradition goes back to Ancient Rome, when plebeians (see page 9) were given the leftovers from richer people's tables. If *guanciale* (pig's cheek) or *trippa alla Romana* (tripe) aren't to your taste, there is also a wide range of delicious vegetable dishes, including stuffed artichokes, grilled peppers and roasted aubergines.

Bars and cafés

On every street and square in Rome there is at least one bar or café, open from early morning until late at night. In some bars there are no seats, and customers lean on the bar to enjoy a morning cappuccino and pastry. Other bars and cafés have chairs and tables arranged on the street. In summer, a popular snack is a *gelato* (ice cream). One Roman speciality is *grattachecche* – freshly grated ice flavoured with fruit syrup.

A restaurant on the ➤ **Piazza** Navona. Many restaurants have tables outside, ideal for long summer evenings when people sit for hours and watch the world go by.

Wine production

The region around Rome (Lazio) produces a large amount of wine, much of which is sold in the city's shops, bars and restaurants. Probably the best-known of these local wines is Frascati, a dry white wine. Many Romans buy their wines in *enoteche*. These are shops that double as wine bars, where the customer can drink a glass of wine and enjoy some delicious snacks.

▲ The famous ice cream restaurant Caffè Giolitti is probably the best-known *gelateria* in Rome, offering a wonderful selection of flavours.

International influences

Although most restaurants in Rome serve traditional Italian food, there are a few places where meals from other cultures are served. The Jewish people of Rome (see page 15) have contributed to Roman cuisine with several dishes including *filetti di baccalà* (deep-fried cod fillets) and *fiori di zucca* (courgette flowers cooked in batter). There are also several North African restaurants around the Termini area and there are now quite a few Chinese and Japanese restaurants across Rome.

ENTERTAINMENT

The Ancient Romans enjoyed going to the Colosseum to watch fights. Modern-day entertainment is much less bloodthirsty, although a match between the city's two rival football teams creates a huge amount of excitement.

▲ The ruined interior of the Colosseum. The arena floor has gone, revealing the underfloor rooms where animals were kept.

Ancient entertainment

One of Rome's best-known ancient sites is the huge **amphitheatre** called the Colosseum, built in 72 AD. The Colosseum held up to 55,000 people and had 80 arches that let the huge crowds in and out easily. Wild animals such as lions, elephants and zebras were kept in cages beneath the central area, awaiting their release – and death – in the arena. **Gladiators**, usually prisoners or slaves, were also a popular attraction. They, too, fought to the death.

Cinemas and film-making

Going to the cinema is a popular pastime in Rome. There are over 80 cinemas in the city. Many have ceilings which can be rolled back in the summer to turn them into open-air venues. The most famous film-making studio in Rome is Cinecittà. It was built in 1937 as one of **Mussolini's** grand projects (see page 17), and for a time had the best film-making facilities in the world outside Hollywood. It became world-famous for films such as *Ben Hur* (1959).

Cinema Farnese is one the many ➤ cinemas in Rome showing the latest international films, dubbed into Italian.

Sport in the city

Football is a passion for many Romans and the city has two home teams, AS Roma and Lazio. They share the Olympic Stadium, which was built for the Olympic Games held in Rome in 1960. During the season, the two teams play at the stadium on alternate Sundays in the Italian Championship League. The Olympic Stadium also hosted the football World Cup which was held in Italy in 1990.

Concert venues

Large classical concerts in Rome take place at the Auditorium of Saint Cecilia, the Italian Forum and the Teatro dell'Opera. Smaller events are performed at places across the city including churches, gardens and ancient ruins. A new auditorium has now opened in the north of the city (see page 43). Rock concerts are held at the Palazzo dello Sport at **EUR** and in the Olympic Stadium. In July Rome hosts a jazz festival at the Italian Forum.

 A football match between Lazio and Parma at Rome's Olympic Stadium. Lazio are wearing the pale blue and white strip.

 The Teatro dell' Opera, one of the main concert halls in Rome. Ballet performances are also staged here.

ROMAEUROPA

The RomaEuropa festival was set up by the French Academy at the Villa Medici (see page 23). Since then it has grown in both size and importance. The month-long festival takes place in the summer and features top-quality dance and theatre. Performances are held in the grounds of the Villa Medici and in other locations around Rome.

MUSEUMS AND GALLERIES

Rome is a city full of museums and galleries, many of them crammed with ancient artefacts and priceless paintings. The Vatican Museums and the museums of the Capitoline are the oldest public museums in the world.

Etruscan art

The **Etruscans** lived in central Italy from the 8th century BC (see page 8). They buried their dead in elaborate tombs with the objects they would need for the afterlife. Many of these tombs have since been **excavated**. The largest collection of Etruscan artefacts is at the National Etruscan Museum in Villa Giulia, a **Renaissance** villa. In the garden of the villa is a reconstruction of an Etruscan temple, built in 1891.

▲ An Etruscan artefact on display at the National Etruscan Museum. This clay head comes from a temple in the ancient Etruscan city of Veii.

Ancient Greece and Rome

There are remains from Ancient Rome all over the city, but especially at the **Forum**. The National Museum of Rome has the largest collection of Roman artefacts, displaying sculptures, mosaics, **frescoes** and coins. The Vatican Museums also have good collections of Greek and Roman art including a *trompe l'oeil* floor mosaic which is designed to look as if it is unswept and covered with litter after a feast.

◀ A Roman **gladiator** fights a lion in this sculpture from the 1st century AD. It is in the National Museum of Rome.

The Vatican Museums

The Vatican Museums were founded in 1506 and contain one of the best art collections in the world. These museums are so huge that it is almost impossible to see them all in one day. The most famous part of the complex is the Sistine Chapel, which has frescoes by **Michelangelo**. There are more frescoes in the Raphael Rooms, decorated by the Italian artist Raphael. An art gallery contains paintings by artists such as Giotto, Fra Angelico, Leonardo da Vinci and Titian. The Vatican Library has a collection of more than 100,000 medieval manuscripts and books.

▲ This painting is *The Creation of Adam* by Michelangelo. It covers the ceiling of the Sistine Chapel in the Vatican.

▲ This head, hand and other fragments are part of a huge statue of Emperor Constantine that once stood in the Roman Forum. The pieces are now in the Capitoline Museums.

Private collections

During the Renaissance and in the following years, many wealthy families in Rome collected magnificent pieces of art to decorate their beautiful palaces. Some of these collections are now open to the public. The best-known is the Doria Pamphilj Gallery which has over 400 paintings including masterpieces by Caravaggio (see page 40) and the Spanish painter Diego Velázquez. Other private collections are at the Palazzo Colonna and the Palazzo Barberini.

UNUSUAL MUSEUMS

The city of Rome has several very unusual museums. One museum is devoted entirely to Italy's famous national dish – pasta. Rome also has a waxworks museum, a folklore museum, a museum that tells the story of the **carabinieri** police force and one that covers the history of the liberation of Rome from **Nazi** forces in 1944.

SPECIAL EVENTS

From celebrations of saints' days to military parades, concert seasons to sporting events, there are special events in Rome all through the year.

▲ The Spanish steps decorated with flowers. At the top of the steps is the church of Trinità dei Monti.

Flower festivals

Romans like to celebrate the arrival of spring. Every April there is a dazzling display of azalea flowers on the Spanish Steps. In August people commemorate a legendary fall of snow. In 352 AD Pope Liberius had a dream in which the Virgin Mary told him to set up a church on a snowy place. There was then a miraculous snowfall on the Esquiline Hill in the middle of summer, so the pope founded the church of Saint Maria Maggiore on the spot. Every year, on 5 August, white petals are showered from the ceiling of the church on to the people below to celebrate this event.

▲ Pilgrims carrying lighted candles make their way to the Colosseum on the evening of Good Friday. The procession is always led by the pope.

Easter

The most important time of year for the Christian Church is Easter. This also marks the beginning of the tourist season in Rome. Thousands of **pilgrims** attend the open-air **Mass** on Palm Sunday in St Peter's Square. On Good Friday a huge service is held in the candle-lit Colosseum, then on Easter Sunday the **pope** reads a speech to the crowds of worshippers in St Peter's Square and across the world.

ROME'S BIRTHDAY

Romans celebrate the legendary founding of their city (see page 8) on the Sunday before 21 April. The main birthday celebrations are held in the Piazza del Campidoglio. Torches are lit and there is a huge and spectacular firework display.

Sporting events

Two major sporting events take place in May. The first is the International Horse Show, a show-jumping event held at the Hippodrome, near the Villa Borghese. Wealthy Romans dress in their smartest clothes to go and watch the horses and their riders who come from all over the world to compete. The second event is the Italian Open Tennis Championship which attracts many world-class tennis stars. It is held in the Olympic Forum.

▲ Horse and rider clear a fence at the International Horse Show, held every year near the Villa Borghese in Rome (see page 18).

▼ Christmas in Rome. This Christmas tree is in the **Piazza** Venezia, in front of the huge Victor Emmanuel Monument.

Saints' days

Several saints' days are given special celebrations in Rome. The city has two **patron saints**, St Paul and St Peter (see page 24), and they are celebrated on 29 June with services in the churches of St Paolo fuori le Mura and St Peter's. On 19 March, St Joseph (the father of Jesus) is remembered in the Trionfale area of Rome. People make special fried batter biscuits known as *bigné*. On 23 June a day devoted to St Giovanni is celebrated. In the evening there is a candlelit procession into the **basilica** of St Giovanni in Laterano.

CITY CHARACTERS

Throughout its history, Rome has attracted famous visitors, for example the English poets Keats and Byron. There have also been many famous Romans over the years.

Giovanni Pierluigi da Palestrina

The composer Palestrina was born in about 1525 in a small town just outside Rome, but lived for most of his life in the city. He was a choirboy at the church of Saint Maria Maggiore and in 1551 became responsible for music in St Peter's. Palestrina composed music for many **popes**, writing 105 settings of the **Mass** service as well as many other pieces of music. His style of music became very famous and his Mass settings are still sung in churches around the world.

▲ The composer Palestrina, whose music influenced later composers such as Bach and Handel.

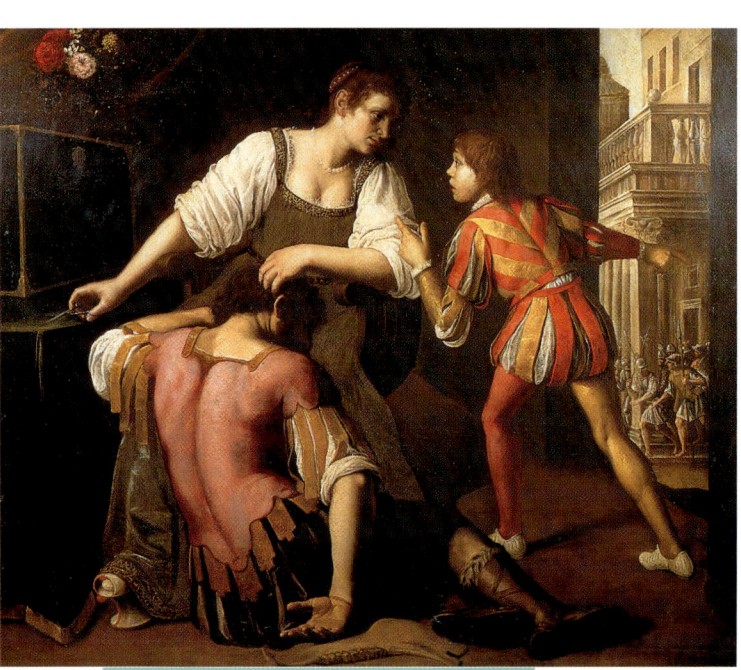

Artemesia Gentileschi's *Samson and Delilah*. Her paintings are full of bold images and colour. ▲

Artemesia Gentileschi

The artist Artemesia Gentileschi was born in Rome in 1593. Her father, Orazio Gentileschi, was also an artist. He was a follower of the Italian painter Michelangelo Merisi da Caravaggio, and he taught Artemesia to appreciate Caravaggio's dramatic style of painting, using brilliant colours and vivid effects of light and shade. Artemesia used Caravaggio's techniques to paint many heroines from the Bible and from mythology. She later moved to Florence, Venice and Naples and became a well-respected artist.

Roberto Rossellini

Roberto Rossellini was one of the most famous cinema directors from Cinecittà studios (see page 34). He was born in Rome in 1906. In the **Second World War** Rossellini secretly recorded the activities of the **Resistance** movement. After the war, in 1945, he used this footage in the film *Roma Città Aperta* (*Rome Open City*) which showed what life was really like during **Nazi** occupation. This film started a new movement in Italian cinema known as **Neo-realism**.

A scene from Roberto Rossellini's film ▲ *Roma Città Aperta.* Rossellini tried to give a realistic picture of life during the war.

Alberto Moravia

Alberto Moravia was born in Rome in 1907. At the age of nine he became ill with **tuberculosis** of the bone and spent the next few years as an invalid. Even though he could not go to school, he learned several languages and read many books. He also started to write. His first novel was published in 1929 and caused a sensation because of its unflattering description of Italian society. Some of his best known works are set in Rome, for example the novel *La Romana* (*The Woman of Rome*). Alberto Moravia died in 1990.

▲ The Roman novelist Alberto Moravia in his study in 1988. He wrote many short stories as well as novels.

Giulio Andreotti

Giulio Andreotti has been prime minister of Italy seven times. Born in Rome in 1919, Andreotti has a reputation as a skilful, powerful and witty politician – his nickname was *la volpe*, 'the fox'. Recently Andreotti has been accused of serious crimes, including involvement in the kidnapping and murder of former Italian prime minister Aldo Moro in 1978. He is also accused of having **Mafia** links.

Giulio Andreotti at ➤ an international meeting in 1991. Andreotti was a politician in the Italian Christian Democratic party.

G. ANDREOTTI

THE FUTURE OF ROME

The future presents problems for Rome. The city needs modernizing but it also has a huge number of ancient sites to preserve.

Traffic problems

Pollution and fumes from Rome's traffic are causing serious damage to ancient monuments. Over the years city councils have looked for ways to cut traffic congestion, but with two million cars on Rome's roads, the problem is a major one. Efforts are being made to improve public transport, but this is not easy. Plans to build a railway line from Rome to Ciampino Airport were dropped when it was found that the line would cut through the remains of a Roman villa. Similar problems have slowed the building of a third Metro line.

▲ Restoration in the Campo de' Fiori. Building work like this is a common sight in central Rome.

Jubilee 2000

The year 2000 is a Holy Year in Rome (see page 25), an event for which the city prepared for a long time. Rome has been given a massive facelift in readiness for the millions of tourists and **pilgrims** coming to the city during 2000. For months, even years, many buildings were covered in scaffolding while being cleaned and restored. Romans had to endure traffic chaos and inconvenience as the city was disrupted by building projects.

◄ In 1999 the exterior of St Peter's was restored. A huge firework display on 30 September celebrated the completion of the work.

New designs

In 1996 building work started on a new **auditorium** designed by the Italian architect, Renzo Piano. As excavations began, remains of a large, 6th-century Roman villa were discovered, so Piano had to rethink the layout of his building. In fact Piano designed three auditoriums. One seats 2,700 people, one is smaller, seating 1,200 people, and the smallest is for 500 people. There is also an outdoor **amphitheatre** which holds up to 3,000 people.

Cinecittà

Film-making is once again thriving in Rome, based at the Cinecittà studios (see page 34). Cinecittà produced many famous films in the years after the **Second World War**, but then fell on hard times. Much of its land was sold and a shopping centre built there. Now, however, Cinecittà is equipped with the latest digital technology and has started to attract film-makers from all over the world.

Francesco Rutelli, mayor of ▲ Rome since 1993. He is a very popular figure in the city.

TREATY OF ROME

In 1957 six countries, including Italy, signed the Treaty of Rome. This treaty was an agreement to co-operate on economic and energy issues and was the start of the European Union. On 1 January 1999 Italy joined the single European currency, the Euro. Italian Euro coins will be issued on 1 January 2002.

▲ Making a film version of *A Midsummer Night's Dream* at the Cinecittà studios.

Political changes

In the early 1990s many Italian government officials were accused of **bribery** and corruption. Some politicians resigned and dozens were arrested. In Rome, too, change swept through the city's council. The **Green Party** won the city elections in 1993 and Francesco Rutelli became mayor. He was re-elected in 1997. Under his leadership, there have been many restoration and cleaning projects in the city, as well as plans to improve public transport.

TIMELINE

This timeline shows some of the most important dates in Rome's history.
All the events are mentioned earlier in the book.

BC

753
Traditional date for the founding of Rome by Romulus

509
Romans overthrow their **Etruscan** rulers
Roman **Republic** is founded

494
Plebeians revolt against patrician rule

450
Roman Law is written down in a code of law, the Twelve Tables, displayed in the **Forum**

264-146
Punic Wars between Rome and Carthage

27
Augustus becomes the first emperor of the **Roman Empire**; he begins to rebuild the city

1ST CENTURY AD

42
Peter and Paul come to Rome

64
Fire destroys a large part of the city, said to have been started by Emperor Nero to clear the slums

67
Peter and Paul are put to death

72-80
Colosseum is built

2ND CENTURY

118-28
Pantheon is built

3RD CENTURY

270s
Emperor Aurelius builds a protective wall around Rome

4TH CENTURY

313
Christians permitted to worship freely in Rome

320s
First **basilica** of St Peter is built

380
Christianity becomes the official religion of the Roman Empire

5TH CENTURY

410
Rome is raided by the **Visigoths**

455
Rome is raided by the **Vandals**

476
Western half of Roman Empire collapses

14TH CENTURY

1300
First Holy Year

1309-77
Pope moves to Avignon

1348
Black Death kills many in Rome

1377-1417
Era known as the **Great Schism**

15TH CENTURY

1417-31

Reign of Pope Martin V and start of **papal** rule in Rome (until 1870)

1447-55

Reign of Pope Nicholas V and start of **Renaissance** in Rome

16TH CENTURY

1506-90s

St Peter's is rebuilt

1527

Rome attacked by armies of Charles V

1556

Jews forced to move into Ghetto

18TH CENTURY

1798

French troops, under the command of **Napoleon**, enter Rome and take control of the city

19TH CENTURY

1814

Papal rule restored in the city

1861

All Italian **states** apart from Rome are united as one country

1870

Italian troops storm Rome; it becomes capital of the unified Italy

1887

Stock market crash ends building work across much of Rome

20TH CENTURY

1922

Fascists, led by **Benito Mussolini**, march on Rome

1929

Lateran Treaty agreed between pope and Mussolini to create the Vatican City State

1937

Building of Cinecittà begins

1943

Arrest of Mussolini; Rome **occupied** by the **Nazis**

1944

Liberation of Rome by Allied forces

1945

Execution of Mussolini

1946

Italy becomes a Republic

1957

Treaty of Rome signed, establishing what is now the European Union

1960

Olympic Games held in Rome

1976

Giulio Andreotti becomes Prime Minister for the first time

1978

Murder of former Prime Minister Aldo Moro

1990

Football World Cup held in Italy

1993

Investigations into government corruption

1993

Francesco Rutelli becomes Rome's first **Green** mayor

1995

Giulio Andreotti goes on trial for associations with the **Mafia**

21ST CENTURY

2000

Jubilee Holy Year in Rome

GLOSSARY

amphitheatre   A circular or oval building with rows of seats arranged around a central area called the arena.

auditorium   The room in a concert hall or theatre where a performance takes place in front of an audience.

basilica   A type of Roman Catholic church. It is a large rectangular building.

Bernini, Gian Lorenzo (1598-1680)   A famous Italian sculptor, artist and architect who designed many buildings and monuments in Rome.

besiege   To surround a city with troops and bombard it into surrender.

Black Death   A type of plague that spread from China to Europe in the 14th century. It was called the Black Death because it caused black marks on the skin.

bribery   Offering someone money or other benefits in order to influence their opinions or actions.

canopy   An ornamental or protective covering erected over an object such as an altar. The *baldacchino* in St Peter's is a huge, ornate canopy made of bronze.

carabinieri   The military police force in Rome.

civil war   A war between different groups within a single country rather than between different countries.

commuter   Someone who travels a distance to work.

concentration camp   A large prison camp. During the Second World War the Nazis set up hundreds of concentration camps, where they killed more than six million people, most of them Jews.

consuls   Two elected officials in Ancient Rome who had the highest authority in the Republic.

dynasty   A family that rules for many generations.

Etruscans   A people who lived in central Italy from about 800 BC. They greatly influenced the Ancient Romans, but fell under Roman power in about 200 BC.

EUR   This stands for Esposizione Universale di Roma (Universal Exhibition of Rome). EUR is a development on the outskirts of Rome which was originally designed as a monument to Fascism in the 1940s. It was finally completed in 1976 and contains houses, offices, museums, a park and the huge Palazzo dello Sport.

excavate   To dig something up, or dig around something buried under the ground, for example ancient ruins.

Fascist   In Italy, the political movement started by Benito Mussolini after the First World War (1914-18). It rapidly gained support in the 1920s. The Fascists promised to restore national pride through military conquests.

Forum   A large open space which was the centre of government, business and economic life in Ancient Rome.

fresco   A wall painting using watercolours on plaster.

gladiator   A soldier in Ancient Rome who was trained to fight in the arena for entertainment.

Great Schism   The period from 1378 to 1417 during which there were rival popes in Avignon and Rome, and at one point also in Pisa.

Green Party   A party that fights for environmental issues.

Greenwich Mean Time   The time in Greenwich, England, which stands on the zero line of longitude. It is used as a base for calculating the time in the rest of the world.

immigrants   People who come to and settle in a country where they were not born and of which they are not citizens.

kosher (of food)   Prepared according to Jewish religious laws.

Lateran Treaty   The agreement made between Pope Pius XI and Benito Mussolini in 1929 which created the Vatican City State. It was named after the Lateran Palace, home of successive popes for hundreds of years.

Mafia   An international criminal organisation from Sicily.

Mass   The main service of the Roman Catholic Church.

Mazzini, Giuseppe (1805-72)   An Italian revolutionary who fought for the unification of Italy.

Michelangelo (1475-1564)   Italian sculptor, painter and architect who worked in Rome. Among his most famous works are the Pietà sculpture in St Peter's and the paintings on the ceiling of the Sistine Chapel.

Mussolini, Benito (1883-1945)   Leader of the Italian Fascist party. Known as 'Il Duce' (The Leader), he became dictator of Italy in 1922. He was killed in 1945.

Napoleon Bonaparte (1769-1821)   French general who led France from 1799. He became emperor of the French Empire in 1804 and ruled until his final defeat in 1815.

Nazi   The name of the Fascist party in Germany which came to power in the 1930s.

Neo-realism   A movement in Italian cinema, started by Roberto Rossellini in the 1940s, which made use of natural settings and gritty portrayals of life.

obelisk   A stone pillar with flat sides that ends in a pyramid-type point. Obelisks are built as monuments in memory of an event or person.

occupied   In wartime, describes a place that is under the control of the enemy.

papal   Relating to the pope.

patron saint   A saint who is a particular guardian of a group of people or a place.

persecute   To mistreat someone because of their beliefs.

piazza   The Italian name for a large open area surrounded by buildings – a square.

pilgrim   A person who makes a journey, called a pilgrimage, to a holy place.

pope   The head of the Roman Catholic Church, also called the Bishop of Rome.

Punic Wars   Three wars between 264-146 BC fought between the Ancient Romans and the Carthaginians.

relic   A treasured object which has survived for many years and which is associated with a saint.

Renaissance   The name given to the period roughly between 1450-1600 when there was a revival of art, literature and learning throughout Europe. The Renaissance started in Italy in the 1400s.

Republic   A country in which the government and head of state are elected by the people.

Resistance, the   The secret organization that fought for liberty in countries occupied by Nazis during the Second World War.

Roman Empire   The territory conquered by the Ancient Romans. The Empire was at its height during the reign of Trajan (98-117 AD).

sack   The plundering and destruction of a city by an invading force.

Second World War   A major war that lasted from 1939 to 1945 and involved many countries. Eventually Germany, Italy and Japan were defeated by Britain, France, the USSR and the USA.

shrine   A place of worship, often associated with a particular person or object.

state   A country or other political unit that governs itself and makes its own laws.

stock exchange   A place where stocks and shares in companies are bought and sold.

stock market crash   A sudden drop in the prices of stocks and shares which causes many people to lose money.

trompe l'oeil   A painting or other work of art which deceives the viewer in some way. The phrase is French for 'deception of the eye'.

tuberculosis   A disease of the lungs which can be fatal.

Vandals   Members of a Germanic tribe who raided the Roman Empire and attacked Rome in 455 AD.

Visigoths   Members of a Germanic tribe who attacked Rome in 410 AD.

INDEX